Burgers

First published in Great Britain in 2006 by Hamlyn
This edition published in 2014 by Spruce
a division of Octopus Publishing Group Ltd
Endeavour House, 189 Shaftesbury Avenue, London, WC2H 8JY
www.octopusbooks.co.uk
www.octopusbooksusa.com

An Hachette UK Company www.hachette.co.uk

Distributed in the US by Hachette Book Group USA
237 Park Avenue, New York NY 10017 USA

Distributed in Canada by Canadian Manda Group
165 Dufferin Street, Toronto, Ontario, Canada M6K 3H6

ISBN 978 1 84601 481 9
A CIP catalogue record for this book is available from the British Library
Printed and bound in China
10 9 8 7 6 5 4 3 2 1

Consultant Publisher Sarah Ford
Author David Morgan
Design Eoghan O'Brien and Michelle Tilly
Photographer Stephen Conroy
Home Economist Sunil Vijayakar
Stylist Rachel Jukes
Production Controller Sarah-Jayne Johnson

Notes

A few recipes include nuts or nut derivatives. It is
advisable for those with known allergic reactions to nuts
and nut derivatives and those who may be potentially
vulnerable to these allergies, such as pregnant and
nursing mothers, invalids, the elderly, babies and
children, to avoid dishes made with nuts and nut
oils. It is also prudent to check the labels of prepared
ingredients for the possible inclusion of nut derivatives.

The American Egg Board advises that eggs should not
be consumed raw. This book contains some dishes made
with raw or lightly cooked eggs. It is prudent for more
vulnerable people such as pregnant and nursing mothers,
invalids, the elderly, babies, and young children to avoid
uncooked or lightly cooked dishes made with eggs.

Whole milk, fresh herbs, and large eggs should be
used unless otherwise stated.

Ovens should be preheated to the specified
temperature—if using a fan-assisted oven, follow the
manufacturer's instructions for adjusting the time and
the temperature.

THE EXCITING VARIETIES ARE ENDLESS!

Burgers

spruce

Contents

introduction

WHAT EXACTLY IS A BURGER?

The dictionary defines a burger as a sandwich consisting of a cooked beef patty in a bun that's often accompanied by a variety of other ingredients. While this is correct, we all know that nowadays the word "burger" covers any number of permutations on this classic staple. Wonderfully versatile, the burger is the ultimate choice for a quick and easy bite on the go, but it also graces the menus of some of the finest eateries. It's fair to say that it's America's—and probably the world's—favorite fast food.

THE VERSATILE SANDWICH

Although beef is traditionally the staple ingredient in a burger, it's by no means the only possibility and, as this book demonstrates, there are endless variations when it comes to making your own burgers. From ground lamb to fish and vegetables, there really are no limits, and then of course there's the decision to be made about which sauce or relish you use and what accompaniments you serve with your burger.

Whether you're eating it from a paper napkin or serving up something special for guests, you'll enjoy searching for your perfect combination and trying out the many classic and unusual burger ideas over the following pages. So, if you thought a burger was just beef in a bun, it's time to think again!

THE HISTORY OF THE BURGER

Although we may think of the burger as being a relatively modern invention, it has, in fact, been enjoyed in various forms for many hundreds of years. It is believed that the great Mongol armies led by Genghis Khan ate meat patties while traveling on their conquering missions. With time being of the essence, they favored food that could be eaten without the need to stop and make camp. These early burgers were convenient because they could easily be eaten with one hand while the armies continued to ride. However, they were consumed raw so they probably didn't have quite the same enjoyment factor that we expect from convenience food nowadays.

THE HAMBURG STEAK

The humble burger became gradually more appetizing over the years although, for a long time, it was still regarded as a convenient way of having a quick and filling meal using the most basic of ingredients. It's believed that the burger was originally introduced to America via the European immigrant ships in the early nineteenth century. Germans travelling to North America from Hamburg ate Hamburg steak on the voyage. It was a popular local food that suited the conditions perfectly because it traveled well and kept for a long time as the meat was generally salted. Hamburg steak was an economical meal, as cheaper cuts of meat were made more appetizing by blending in various spices and flavorings. To make the meat go even further on board ship, other ingredients such as bread crumbs were added and the meat patties were seared and served with bread, like a sandwich. On their arrival in America, the new immigrants kept their culinary traditions alive and the popularity of these Hamburg steaks began to spread. The name evolved into the hamburger and a great American tradition was born.

A LASTING INFLUENCE

The hamburger became popular at fairs and markets with stalls being set up all over the country and it wasn't long before franchises and retail outlets were opened that sold only the popular food. Today, a town without a burger bar is a rare sight indeed, and the burger is still top of most people's quick-fix food list. As the burger gained in popularity so new variations began to crop up and people became a little more adventurous.

CREATING A CLASSIC

Ground beef can take other flavors well and it is easily combined with herbs, spices, and flavorings before being shaped and cooked. Of course, the most popular addition to the burger was cheese and this is still the most widely consumed variation of the classic burger today. Relishes and accompaniments were also easy to add as the burger was eaten in a bun, generally with the hands, and anything that could be packed comfortably into the bun was considered appropriate. So, salad, mayonnaise, tomato relish, mustard, gherkins, and onions all became regular companions to the beef burger. At the same time, individuals set about creating their own burger mixtures by seasoning and flavoring the meat in different ways to create ever more interesting takes on the basic burger.

Today, this national favorite is just as likely to be found at a stall by the side of the road as on the menu of a top restaurant and both will provide an equally enjoyable

experience. In fact, in recent years, the burger has experienced a surge of popularity in restaurants, with a greater appreciation of its place in the American culinary heritage. Chefs have begun to realize the potential of this much-loved meal with its humble origins. The burger is often used as a quality benchmark for restaurants—get this right and you can rely on a loyal customer following.

MAKING YOUR OWN BURGERS

You may well enjoy treating yourself to a burger and fries for lunch every now and again but it's fair to say that nothing can compare to the taste of a freshly cooked, homemade burger with all the trimmings. You have total control over the ingredients used, the quality and cut of the meat, and the cooking technique and time. And let's not forget that making burgers is fun— from mixing the ingredients to shaping the patties and your mouth beginning to water as the smells waft

from the grill, there's something immensely satisfying about tucking into your own homemade burgers.

HANDS-ON FOOD

Kids love to get involved as making burgers can be a gloriously messy experience that requires getting your hands covered in food; they're also a great way to introduce children to new ingredients. Perhaps the most exciting thing about making your own burgers is that the variations are endless. There's no need to miss out if you're a vegetarian or you don't eat red meat. As this book demonstrates, there's a burger recipe to suit every taste. How about trying a Sweet Potato, Lima Bean, and Feta Burger with Sun-blushed Tomato Pesto (see page 51)? Or get creative with a Crispy Tofu Burger (see page 52). If you are a meat lover then there's no need to limit yourself to beef. You'll find ideas for pork, lamb, and chicken burgers as well as some great ideas for fish such as the Swordfish Steak Burger with a Crunchy Orange Salsa (see page 45).

QUICK AND CONVENIENT

As well as being extremely versatile, homemade burgers can provide healthy and nutritious meals that score high on the convenience factor, too. Many of the recipes in this book can be prepared in advance and cooked to order. In fact, a lot of the beef and other meat-based burgers will benefit from standing in the refrigerator to chill before cooking—as this allows the patties to set and makes them easier to handle. As most of the recipes are quick to cook, you'll spend less time in the kitchen later on.

COOKING TECHNIQUES

Burgers have long been associated with barbecues and they're ideal for throwing on the grill. Condiments, relishes, and accompaniments can all be set out for people to help themselves and the smoky flavor really does enhance the taste of the burger. This is true of fish and many vegetarian burgers, as well as meat. The combination of ground meat with other ingredients such as bread crumbs or egg to bind the mixture together means that the burger is firm enough to withstand the high temperatures and rough treatment that barbecuing entails. Obviously, not all recipes are suited to this cooking technique and some of the more delicate burgers require gentler handling. These can be cooked just as easily with a little oil in a griddle or skillet for equally delicious results.

Glossary

US	UK
all-purpose flour	plain flour
arugula	rocket
bacon slices	bacon rashers
beet	beetroot
bell pepper	sweet pepper
broiler	grill
cilantro	fresh coriander
cornstarch	cornflour
ground beef	minced beef
Lima beans	butterbeans
peanut oil	groundnut oil
scallions	spring onions
shrimps	prawns
skillet	frying pan
superfine sugar	caster sugar
zucchini	courgette

Conversion Table

Standard American cup measurements are used in all recipes.

¼ **cup =** 60 ml (2 fl oz)
⅓ **cup =** 75 ml (3 fl oz)
½ **cup =** 120 ml (4 fl oz)
1 cup = 240 ml (8 fl oz)

1 cup dried bread crumbs = 125 g (4 oz)
1 cup fresh bread crumbs = 60 g (2 oz)

Classic American

2 lb good quality coarsely ground beef
2 garlic cloves, crushed
8 bacon slices
a little light olive oil, for brushing
salt and pepper

To serve:

4 large burger buns
2 cups mixed salad leaves
1 beefsteak tomato, sliced
4 thick slices strong cheddar cheese
or Monterery Jack
1 small red onion, sliced into rings
1 quantity of Quick BBQ Sauce (*see page 63*)

THIS ONE IS FOR ADULTS ONLY; WITH A FULL HALF POUND OF BURGER PER PERSON IT'S A HEARTY MEAL FOR ANY MEAT LOVER.

1. Mix the beef and garlic together and season well with salt and pepper. Divide the mixture into 4 equal portions and form each one into a round patty, pressing together firmly. Cover and chill for at least 30 minutes.

2. Broil the bacon until slightly crisp and keep warm. Heat a griddle pan or barbecue to medium-high. Brush the burgers with a little oil and cook them for 5–6 minutes on each side, depending on how you like them cooked.

3. Assemble each burger by covering the base of each bun first with salad leaves then tomato slices. Place the cooked burger on the salad then top with the cheese, bacon, and sliced red onion. Serve open or topped with the bun lid and accompanied with lots of Quick BBQ Sauce.

SICILIAN BURGER

1 tablespoon vegetable oil
1 red onion, finely chopped
3 garlic cloves
1¼ lb good quality coarsely ground beef
2 tablespoons chopped basil
2 tablespoons chopped marjoram
2 tablespoons chopped oregano
⅓ cup freshly grated Parmesan cheese
3 oz sun-dried tomatoes, finely chopped
½ cup black olives, finely chopped
a little light olive oil, for brushing
salt and pepper

To serve:

2 soft focaccia rolls, quartered
Basil Mayonnaise (*see page 61*)
2 cups arugula
1 ball of mozzarella cheese, about 4 oz
a small bunch of basil

1. Heat the oil in a skillet and fry the onion and garlic over a medium heat for 4 minutes or until softened. Set aside to cool. Place the beef, onion and garlic mixture, herbs, Parmesan, tomatoes, and olives in a large bowl. Season with salt and pepper and mix well. Divide the mixture into 8 portions and shape each one into a ball then flatten slightly into a burger. Cover and chill for 30 minutes.

2. Heat a griddle pan or barbecue to hot. Brush the burgers with a little oil and cook them for 4–5 minutes on each side until slightly charred on the outside and medium in the center.

3. Split the focaccia rolls in half and toast slightly on the griddle pan or barbecue. Spread the base with basil mayonnaise and top with arugula and the cooked burger. Tear the mozzarella ball into pieces and divide among the 8 burgers. Top with the lids and a basil leaf and secure with a toothpick. Serve with extra basil mayonnaise and arugula.

Blue-Cheese BURGER

1 tablespoon vegetable oil
1 onion, finely chopped
2 garlic cloves, crushed
1¼ lb good quality coarsely ground beef
2 tablespoons finely chopped chives
1 pear, peeled, cored and grated
1 tablespoon wholegrain mustard
2 tablespoons butter
3 large mushrooms, thickly sliced
5 oz blue cheese
a little light olive oil, for brushing
salt and pepper

To serve:
4 thick slices walnut bread
1 bunch watercress
a few chopped chives

1. Heat the oil in a skillet and cook the onion and garlic over a medium heat for about 5 minutes or until softened. Set aside to cool. Mix together the ground beef, the onion and garlic mixture, chives, pear, and mustard. Season well with salt and pepper.

2. Divide the mix into 4 equal portions. Form into balls then flatten slightly. Cover and chill for at least 30 minutes.

3. Melt the butter in a small pan and add the mushrooms. Fry for about 5 minutes then set aside to cool. Heat a griddle pan to hot. Brush the burgers with a little oil and cook them for about 5 minutes on each side, depending on how well you like them done. Divide the blue cheese into 4 portions; place them on the top of each burger then melt slightly under a hot broiler.

4. To assemble, toast the walnut bread slices on a hot griddle pan until lightly browned. Top each slice with the fried mushrooms and a burger. Garnish with the watercress and chives and serve immediately.

Mexico City
BURGER WITH AVOCADO SALSA

1 tablespoon light olive oil, plus extra for brushing
1 onion, finely chopped
2½ tablespoons taco seasoning
1¼ lb good quality coarsely ground beef
2 tablespoons chopped cilantro
1 oz jalapeño peppers
1 teaspoon Tabasco sauce
salt and pepper

Avocado salsa:
1 avocado, peeled and diced
2 large tomatoes, skinned, seeded, and diced
1 red chili, seeded and finely chopped
4 scallions, thinly shredded
2 tablespoons chopped cilantro
juice and grated zest of 1 lime
3 tablespoons olive oil

To serve:
4 soft tortillas
iceberg lettuce, shredded
4 tablespoons sour cream

1. Heat the oil in a skillet and cook the onion with the taco seasoning until soft, about 3–4 minutes. Leave to cool then season with salt and pepper and mix with the beef, cilantro, jalapeño peppers, and Tabasco sauce. Divide the mixture into 8 portions, shape each into a ball and flatten out a little. Cover and chill for at least 30 minutes.

2. Meanwhile, combine all the ingredients for the salsa in a small bowl. Chill to allow the flavors to develop.

3. Heat a griddle pan or barbecue to hot. Brush the burgers with a little oil and cook them for up to 5 minutes on each side, depending on how well you like them done.

4. Warm the tortillas under a broiler. Place some of the lettuce over each tortilla then add two of the mini burgers. Top with a few spoonfuls of salsa and a dollop of sour cream. Fold the tortillas in half and serve.

The Ultimate CHEESE BURGER

1¼ lb good quality ground beef
2 oz quince paste, finely diced
2 tablespoons chopped parsley
1 tablespoon Dijon mustard
1 teaspoon cayenne pepper
1 tablespoon Worcestershire sauce
½ cup freshly grated Parmesan cheese
a little light olive oil, for brushing
6 oz mature cheddar cheese, cut into thick slices
salt and pepper

To serve:
4 crusty rolls
salad leaves
1 beefsteak tomato, sliced
a selection of pickles, such as gherkins and pickled onions
1 quantity Wholegrain Mustard Mayonnaise
(*see page 61*)

FRESH QUINCE HAS A FLAVOR SOMEWHERE BETWEEN AN APPLE AND A PEAR; BECAUSE OF ITS HIGH PECTIN CONTENT IT MAKES EXCELLENT PRESERVES AND PASTES. QUINCE PASTE IS SWEET WITH A DELICATE FLOWERY TASTE AND IS FOUND IN GOURMET MARKETS.

1. Mix together the beef, quince paste, parsley, mustard, cayenne pepper, Worcestershire sauce, and Parmesan in a large bowl. Season well with salt and pepper and divide into 4 portions. Form them into balls and flatten slightly into burgers. Cover and chill for 30 minutes.

2. Heat a griddle pan to hot. Brush the burgers with a little oil and cook for about 5 minutes on each side, depending on how well you like them done. Divide the slices of cheese over the burgers and melt slightly under a hot broiler.

3. To assemble, halve the rolls and toast under a broiler and top each base with salad leaves and tomato slices followed by a burger and the lid. Serve immediately with a selection of pickles and wholegrain mustard mayonnaise on the side.

Aussie Burger

WITH THE LOT!

1¼ lb good quality coarsely ground beef
2 garlic cloves, crushed
1 onion, finely chopped
1 tablespoon Dijon mustard
1 tablespoon chopped thyme
1 tablespoon Worcestershire sauce
4 Canadian bacon slices
a little light olive oil, for brushing
4 small eggs
salt and pepper

To serve:
4 burger buns
mixed salad leaves
4 thin slices cheddar cheese
4 slices pineapple
8 slices of pickled beet, crinkle cut
1 quantity Southern Fried Onion Rings
(*see page 57*)

1. Mix the beef, garlic, onion, mustard, thyme, and Worcestershire sauce together and season. Divide the mixture into 4 equal portions and shape into balls then flatten into burgers. Cover and chill for 1 hour.

2. Broil the bacon until slightly crisp and keep warm. Heat a griddle pan to medium-high. Brush the burgers with a little oil and cook them for about 5 minutes on each side, depending on how well you like them done.

3. Heat some oil in a skillet and fry the eggs for 3–4 minutes or until the white part is cooked but the yolk is still soft. Meanwhile, halve and toast the rolls under a broiler.

4. To assemble, layer some salad leaves, the burger, bacon, cheddar, pineapple, beet, and egg on the base of each bun and top with the lid. Stick a skewer through the burger to prevent it falling apart and serve topped with the onion rings.

CHILI-BEEF TOPPED BURGER

1 lb good quality ground beef
5 oz pork and herb sausages, skinned
1 garlic clove, crushed
1 tablespoon Dijon mustard
2 tablespoons finely chopped parsley
a little light olive oil, for brushing
salt and pepper

Chili sauce:
1 tablespoon light olive oil
1 onion, finely chopped
1 large red chili, finely chopped
1 teaspoon paprika
1 garlic clove, crushed
7 oz ground beef
1¾ cups pureed tomatoes
1 tablespoon Worcestershire sauce
1 teaspoon Tabasco sauce
7 oz can red kidney beans, drained and rinsed

To serve:
4 ciabatta rolls
salad leaves

1. First, make the chili sauce. Heat the oil in a skillet and cook the onion, chili, paprika, and garlic until soft, about 3–4 minutes. Add the ground beef and cook for 2–3 minutes until browned. Stir through the remaining sauce ingredients then season with salt and pepper and stir well. Cover and cook over a low heat for 20 minutes.

2. To make the burger, mix together the beef, sausage-meat, garlic, mustard, and parsley in a bowl. Season well with salt and pepper and divide into 4 equal portions. Form into balls then flatten into burgers. Cover and chill for 30 minutes.

3. Heat a griddle pan or barbecue to hot. Brush the burgers with a little oil and cook for about 5 minutes on each side, depending on how well you like them done.

4. To assemble, halve the rolls and toast under a broiler. Top each base with salad leaves followed by a burger. Spoon over the chili sauce and serve with the roll lid on the side.

Indian Spiced

WITH MANGO CHUTNEY

2 tablespoons light olive oil, plus extra for brushing
1 onion, finely chopped
2 garlic cloves, crushed
1 red chili, seeded and finely chopped
1 teaspoon black mustard seeds
1 tablespoon garam masala
1 teaspoon turmeric
1¼ lb ground lamb
1 cup bread crumbs
1 small egg
salt and pepper

To serve:
8 mini naan breads
a small bunch of cilantro, chopped
red chili powder (optional)
½ cucumber, cubed
2 tomatoes, cubed
mango chutney
mini pappadoms

1. Heat the oil in a skillet and fry the onion, garlic, chili, mustard seeds, and spices for 5 minutes or until the onion has softened and the mustard seeds start to pop. Set aside to cool.

2. Mix together the lamb, bread crumbs, egg, and onion mixture in a large bowl. Season with salt and pepper then divide into 8 portions. Form them into round balls and flatten slightly into burgers. Cover and chill for at least 30 minutes.

3. Heat a griddle pan or barbecue to hot. Brush the burgers with a little oil and cook for 5 minutes on each side depending on how well you like them done.

4. To assemble, gently heat the naan breads in a hot oven. Top with some cilantro, a sprinkle of red chili powder, if using, a burger, and the cucumber and tomato. Serve with mango chutney and mini pappadoms.

GREEK-STYLE LAMB BURGER

1¼ lb good quality coarsely ground lamb
2 garlic cloves, crushed
grated zest of 1 lemon
5 oz feta cheese, diced
⅓ cup black olives, chopped
½ cup pine nuts, dry-roasted and chopped
3 tablespoons chopped oregano
a little light olive oil, for brushing
salt and pepper

Salad:

3 tomatoes, cut into wedges
½ cucumber, cut into ribbons
with a vegetable peeler
⅓ cup Kalamata olives
1 tablespoon chopped flat leaf parsley

To serve:

4 floured rolls
pine nuts
Greek or whole milk plain yogurt
lemon wedges

1. Mix together all the ingredients for the burger in a bowl and season well. Divide the mix into 4 equal portions and form into balls then flatten slightly into burgers. Cover and chill for at least 30 minutes.

2. Heat a griddle pan or barbecue to hot. Brush the burgers with a little oil and cook for about 5 minutes on each side, depending on how well you like them done.

3. Halve the rolls and toast under a broiler. Top each base with some salad, the burgers, and pine nuts and serve with yogurt and lemon wedges.

JERK PORK BURGER
WITH MANGO SALSA

1¼ lb good quality coarsely ground pork
2 tablespoons jerk seasoning
grated zest of 1 lime
1 inch piece of fresh ginger root, peeled and grated
2 garlic cloves, crushed
4 scallions, finely chopped
1 tablespoon thyme
a little light olive oil, for brushing
salt and pepper

Mango salsa:
1 mango, peeled, cored and finely diced
½ red onion, finely diced
1 red chili, seeded and finely diced
2 tablespoons chopped mint
1 tablespoon chopped cilantro
2 tablespoons olive oil
grated zest and juice of 1 lime

To serve:
4 burger buns
salad leaves
4 large pieces of marinated roasted red bell pepper
1 quantity Cajun Sweet Potato Fries
(see page 56)

1. Mix together all the ingredients for the burger in a large bowl. Season well with salt and pepper then divide into 4 equal portions. Shape into balls and flatten slightly into burgers. Cover and chill for 30 minutes.

2. To make the salsa, mix together all the ingredients and set aside for at least 30 minutes at room temperature to allow the flavors to develop.

3. Heat a griddle pan or barbecue to hot. Brush the burgers with a little oil and cook them for 5 minutes on each side depending on how well you like them done.

4. To assemble, cut the buns in half and toast lightly on the griddle pan or barbecue. Top each base with salad leaves, roasted peppers, and a burger. Spoon over the salsa and top with the lid. Serve with the Cajun sweet potato fries.

ENGLISH BREAKFAST
B U R G E R

THIS IS THE ULTIMATE BREAKFAST ON THE GO. IT'S GREAT SERVED WITH ENGLISH BREAKFAST TEA.

1 lb good quality thick pork sausages
3 tablespoons chopped chives
1 teaspoon powdered English mustard
a little flour, to dust
a little light olive oil, for frying
salt and pepper

To serve:
8 bacon slices
4 slices of black pudding
or blood sausage (optional)
4 eggs
4 English muffins
1 quantity Tomato Ketchup
(*see page 60*)

1. Remove the skins from the sausages and discard. Place the meat in a bowl with the chives and powdered mustard. With floured hands, shape the mixture into 4 thin burgers.

2. Cook the bacon and black pudding, if using, under a preheated broiler until cooked through and slightly crisp, about 5 minutes. Set aside and keep warm.

3. Heat a little oil in a nonstick skillet and cook the sausage burgers for 4 minutes on each side or until cooked through and golden brown. Remove from the pan and drain on paper towels.

4. In the same pan, add a little more oil and fry the eggs for 3–4 minutes or until the white is cooked but the yolk is soft.

5. To assemble, layer the burger, bacon, black pudding, and egg between halved toasted muffins. Serve with tomato ketchup.

PORK SAUSAGE
BURGER
WITH POTATO ROSTI AND BALSAMIC ROASTED ONIONS

7 oz rindless pork belly, chopped
14 oz ground pork
2 teaspoons mace
2 tablespoons chopped rosemary
½ teaspoon cayenne pepper
grated zest of 1 lemon
a little light olive oil, for brushing

Roasted balsamic onions:
2 red onions, cut into quarters
a dash of olive oil
2 tablespoons balsamic vinegar
a few sprigs of thyme

Potato rosti:
2 potatoes, peeled and coarsely grated
2 garlic cloves, crushed
2 tablespoons light olive oil
2 tablespoons unsalted butter

To serve:
mixed salad leaves
a small bunch of rosemary

1. Place the pork belly in a food processor and blitz until finely chopped. Combine with the pork, mace, rosemary, cayenne pepper, and lemon zest, and season with salt and pepper. Divide into 4 equal portions and shape each into a ball. Flatten slightly then cover and chill for 30 minutes.

2. Toss the red onions with a dash of olive oil and the balsamic vinegar in a roasting tin. Sprinkle with the thyme and cook in a preheated oven, 375°F, for 30 minutes or until slightly charred around the edges.

3. When the onions are done, turn the oven up to 425°F. Place the grated potato on a clean dish towel and squeeze out any excess moisture. Transfer to a bowl and add the garlic. Mix thoroughly and season well. Shape the mixture into 4 flat disks. Heat the oil and butter in a pan and fry the rostis for 2 minutes on each side or until lightly browned. Transfer to an ovenproof dish and bake until crisp, about 10 minutes.

4. Heat a griddle pan to medium-high. Brush the burgers with oil and cook for 5 minutes on each side or until they are cooked through.

5. To assemble, place the salad leaves on the rostis and top with a burger, a spoonful of roasted onions, and a sprig of rosemary.

TURKEY AND CHESTNUT BURGER
WITH CRANBERRY AND BRIE

1 tablespoon olive oil
1 onion, chopped
2 garlic cloves, crushed
½ cup chestnuts, roughly chopped
2 tablespoons chopped thyme
1¼ lb coarsely ground turkey
1 cup fresh bread crumbs
1 egg
1 tablespoon cranberry sauce
a little light olive oil, for brushing
salt and pepper

To serve:
4 burger buns
4 oz Brie cheese
4 tablespoons cranberry sauce
salad leaves

1. Heat the oil in a pan and fry the onion and garlic for 4 minutes or until the onion has softened. Remove from the heat and add the chestnuts and thyme. Set aside to cool.

2. Put the turkey, bread crumbs, egg, cranberry sauce, chestnuts, thyme, and onion mixture in a large bowl. Season with salt and pepper and mix well. Divide into 4 equal portions and form each one into a round ball. Flatten slightly into burgers then cover and chill for at least 30 minutes.

3. Heat a griddle pan to medium-high. Brush the burgers with a little oil and cook for 6 minutes on each side or until cooked through.

4. Slice the Brie into 4 pieces and place one on each burger. Melt under a hot broiler then put each one in a toasted bun and top with cranberry sauce. Serve with salad leaves.

Chicken Caesar
BURGER

YOU CAN BUY GOOD CAESAR DRESSING THESE DAYS, SO THERE'S NO NEED TO MAKE YOUR OWN. GET THE BEST QUALITY YOU CAN, THOUGH.

1 lb coarsely ground chicken breast
2 garlic cloves, crushed
1 bunch of scallions, finely chopped
grated zest of 1 lemon
⅓ cup freshly grated Parmesan cheese
2 anchovies, chopped
8 bacon slices
a little light olive oil, for brushing
salt and pepper

To serve:
1 tablespoon olive oil
4 small French baguettes, cut in half lengthwise
1 small romaine lettuce, separated into leaves
Caesar salad dressing
Parmesan cheese shavings

1. Mix together all the ingredients for the burger, except the bacon, in a bowl and season with salt and pepper. Divide the mixture into 4 balls and flatten slightly into burgers. Wrap each one in 2 slices of bacon then cover and chill for at least 30 minutes.

2. Heat a griddle pan or barbecue to medium. Brush the burgers with a little oil and cook them for about 5 minutes on each side or until cooked through.

3. To assemble, brush the insides of the baguettes with oil and toast under a hot broiler until golden. Top each one with lettuce leaves and drizzle with some dressing. Place a burger on the salad and top with shaved Parmesan.

ROAST CHICKEN **BURGER**

WITH SAGE AND ONION STUFFING

2 garlic cloves, crushed
2 tablespoons chopped flat leaf parsley
1 tablespoon olive oil
4 small chicken breasts, skin on
salt and pepper

Sage and onion stuffing:
1 tablespoon light olive oil, plus extra for greasing
1 onion, finely chopped
4 pork sausages
4 tablespoons chopped sage
2 cups fresh bread crumbs
1 egg, beaten

To serve:
4 crusty rolls
iceberg lettuce, shredded

1. First make the stuffing. Heat the oil in a skillet and cook the onion until soft but not browned, about 4 minutes. Remove from the heat and allow to cool slightly. Remove the skins from the sausages and mix the meat with the cooked onion, sage, bread crumbs, and egg. Divide the mixture into 8 pieces, shape them into 8 burger-shaped rounds and place in a lightly greased roasting pan.

2. Mix together the garlic, parsley, and oil and brush over the chicken breasts. Place them in a roasting pan and season well with salt and pepper.

3. Roast both the stuffing and chicken in a preheated oven, 400°F, for 35 minutes or until golden brown and cooked through.

4. To assemble, halve the rolls and toast under a broiler. Top each base with shredded lettuce then 2 stuffing burgers and a roasted chicken breast. Serve immediately with the lid on the side.

Wild Mushroom CHICKEN BURGER
WITH TARRAGON

THIS WONDERFULLY TASTY BURGER IS REALLY ENHANCED BY THE FLAVOR OF THE WILD MUSHROOMS SO DON'T STINT ON THEM—USE MORE IF YOU THINK THE SAUCE NEEDS THEM.

13 oz skinless, boneless chicken thigh, roughly chopped

7 oz skinless, boneless chicken breast, roughly chopped

1 onion, finely chopped

2 garlic cloves, crushed

3 tablespoons chopped tarragon

1 tablespoon Dijon mustard

a little light olive oil, for frying

Mushroom sauce:
2 tablespoons butter

8 oz mixed wild mushrooms, roughly chopped

1 teaspoon wholegrain mustard

1 tablespoon red wine vinegar

½ cup crème fraîche or sour cream

To serve:
4 crusty rolls

1 cup arugula

1. Place the chicken thigh and breast meat in a food processor and blitz until roughly chopped; add the onion, garlic, tarragon, and mustard and blitz for an additional 2 seconds until combined. Divide the mixture into 4 portions and shape into burgers. Cover and chill for 30 minutes.

2. Heat the oil in a skillet and fry the burgers over a medium heat for 6 minutes on each side or until golden and slightly crisp. Remove the burgers from the pan and keep them warm.

3. Melt the butter in the same pan and gently cook the mushrooms for 4–5 minutes until cooked. Stir in the mustard, vinegar, and crème fraîche or sour cream and cook for 1–2 minutes or until the sauce is thick enough to coat the back of a spoon.

4. To assemble, halve the rolls and toast lightly then top each base with arugula followed by a burger. Spoon the wild mushroom sauce over the top and serve with the bun lid on the side.

STICKY LEMON GRASS BURGER

PUREED LEMON GRASS GIVES THIS DISH A WONDERFUL FLAVOR AND IS WELL WORTH SEEKING OUT. IT CAN BE BOUGHT IN JARS FROM SPECIALTY ASIAN STORES.

7 oz skinless, boneless chicken breast, chopped
13 oz skinless, boneless chicken thigh, chopped
1 bunch of scallions, finely chopped
2 tablespoons lemon grass puree
1 inch piece of fresh ginger root, peeled and grated
2 garlic cloves, crushed
3 tablespoons chopped cilantro
2 tablespoons light olive oil
1 tablespoon dark soy sauce
1 tablespoon fish sauce
1 tablespoon rice wine vinegar
1 tablespoon water
2 tablespoons superfine sugar

To serve:
4 crusty chili flake rolls
4 scallions, shredded
¼ cucumber, cut into thin sticks
8 large basil leaves
8 large mint leaves
a small bunch of cilantro
4 lime wedges

1. Place the chicken thigh and breast meat in a food processor and blitz until roughly chopped. Add the scallions, lemon grass, ginger, garlic, and cilantro then blitz for an additional 2 seconds until combined. Divide the mixture into 4 and form into burgers. Cover and chill for 30 minutes.

2. Heat the oil in a shallow skillet and fry the burgers for 4 minutes on each side until golden and slightly crisp. Add the soy sauce, fish sauce, vinegar, water, and sugar and stir until the sugar dissolves. Cover with a lid and cook for a further 3 minutes, turning the burgers occasionally, until the sauce is slightly sticky and the chicken is cooked through.

3. To assemble, halve the rolls and toast. Cover each base with scallions, cucumber, and herbs then place a sticky chicken burger on top. Serve with wedges of lime and the lid on the side.

CHICKEN BURGER
with Goat Cheese

4 skinless chicken breasts
2 tablespoons chopped thyme
2 garlic cloves, crushed
4 thin slices prosciutto
a little light olive oil, for brushing
5 oz goat cheese

Honey-roasted figs:
6 figs, cut into quarters
2 tablespoons olive oil
2 tablespoons orange blossom honey
salt and pepper

To serve:
4 caraway seed rolls
2 cups arugula
extra arugula leaves or thyme sprigs

MAKE SURE YOU GET GOAT CHEESE WITH A RIND, RATHER THAN PACKAGED SOFT GOAT CHEESE. IT HAS A RICHER FLAVOR AND WILL MELT MORE PLEASINGLY OVER THE BURGER.

1. First, cook the honey-roasted figs. Place the figs in a roasting dish and drizzle with the olive oil and honey. Season well with salt and pepper and roast in a preheated oven, 400°F, for 10 minutes until the figs just start to brown.

2. Meanwhile, sandwich each chicken breast between 2 sheets of plastic wrap and flatten slightly with a rolling pin or meat mallet. Rub the thyme and garlic into the chicken, season with salt and pepper and wrap with the prosciutto.

3. Heat a griddle pan or barbecue to medium. Brush the chicken with oil and cook for about 8 minutes on each side or until cooked through. Top each breast with a slice of goat cheese and melt slightly under a hot broiler.

4. To assemble, halve the rolls and toast under a broiler, top each base with arugula leaves and a chicken breast. Spoon the honey-roasted figs over each burger and garnish with extra arugula leaves or thyme sprigs and serve the lids on the side.

PARMESAN-CRUSTED
COD BURGER
WITH LEMON MAYO

1 egg
1 teaspoon powdered English mustard
1½ cups fresh bread crumbs
2 tablespoons finely chopped basil
3 tablespoons freshly grated Parmesan cheese
4 tablespoons all-purpose flour
4 cod fillets, about 6 oz each
2 tablespoons light olive oil
salt and pepper

To serve:
4 crusty poppy seed rolls
mixed salad leaves
1 beefsteak tomato, sliced
4 tablespoons Lemon Mayonnaise (*see page 61*)
lemon wedges

1. First make the crust for the fish. Beat the egg and mustard with a little salt and pepper. Mix together the bread crumbs, basil, and Parmesan in a bowl then turn out onto a plate. Spread the flour on a separate plate.

2. Coat the cod fillets in the flour and dip them first in the egg mixture then coat evenly in the bread crumb mixture.

3. Heat the oil in a shallow pan and fry the fish until golden and cooked through, about 4 minutes on each side.

4. Halve the rolls and toast under a broiler then cover each base with a few salad leaves, tomato slices, and crusted cod fillets. Serve with the lids on the side and lemon mayonnaise, lemon wedges, and extra salad.

CAJUN FISH
BURGER

1¼ lb white fish fillet
1 cup fresh bread crumbs
1 small onion, grated
1 garlic clove
1 egg yolk
1 teaspoon Tabasco sauce
a little light olive oil, for frying

Cajun spice mix:
3 teaspoons paprika
1 teaspoon cayenne pepper
1 teaspoon dried thyme
1 teaspoon dried parsley
1 teaspoon dried oregano
½ teaspoon onion salt
a pinch of cinnamon

To serve:
4 crusty rolls
salad leaves
1 quantity Lima Bean, Tomato,
and Cilantro Salsa (*see page 63*)

1. Heat a small skillet, add all the ingredients for the Cajun spice mix and cook for 1 minute until the spices start to smoke slightly. This will enhance their flavors. Set aside to cool.

2. Skin the fish then chop roughly. Put it in a food processor with the bread crumbs, onion, garlic, egg yolk, Tabasco, and spice mix and blitz until thoroughly blended and the mixture holds together. Don't overblend as you want the fish to have some texture.

3. With slightly wet hands, divide the mixture into 4 equal portions; shape them into balls then flatten into burgers. Cover and chill for 1 hour.

4. Heat the oil in a shallow pan and fry the burgers over a medium-high heat for 5 minutes on each side or until golden and cooked through.

5. To assemble, halve the rolls and toast under a broiler. Place a little salad on the base and top with a burger. Spoon over some of the salsa and serve immediately with the lid on the side.

Beer-battered FISH BURGER

3½ oz all-purpose flour
a pinch of baking powder
¾ cup lager
vegetable oil, for deep frying
4 cod fillets, about 6 oz each
salt and pepper

To serve:
4 crusty rolls
a little butter, for spreading
salad leaves
1 quantity Mixed Herb Mayonnaise (*see page 61*)
1 quantity Tomato Ketchup (*see page 60*)
homemade fries (optional)

ALTHOUGH IT'S DELICIOUS, IF YOU DON'T HAVE THE TIME TO MAKE YOUR OWN KETCHUP THE BOUGHT VARIETY IS FINE FOR THIS RECIPE.

1. To make the batter, beat together the flour, baking powder, and beer to make a smooth batter. Season with salt and pepper and leave to rest in the refrigerator for 20 minutes.

2. Half-fill a large pan or deep-fat fryer with the oil and heat to 350ºF or until a cube of bread browns in 30 seconds.

3. Dip the cod fillets into the batter, shake off any excess and cook in the oil for 5 minutes or until golden brown and cooked through. (You may need to do this in 2 batches or more depending on the size of your pan. Never over-fill a pan of hot oil.) Drain on plenty of paper towels.

4. To assemble, halve and butter the crusty rolls. Fill with salad leaves and the battered fish. Top with the mixed herb mayonnaise and serve with tomato ketchup and homemade fries, if liked.

Sesame Salmon

BURGER

8 tablespoons sesame seeds
4 tablespoons black sesame seeds
4 salmon fillets, about 5 oz each, skinned
2 tablespoons olive oil
1 tablespoon roasted sesame oil

To serve:
2 sesame seed rolls
½ cucumber, cut into ribbons with a vegetable peeler
1 small red onion, finely sliced

THE BLACK SESAME SEEDS GIVE A REAL PROFESSIONAL RESTAURANT LOOK TO THIS BURGER; YOU CAN BUY THEM IN MOST JAPANESE OR INDIAN MARKETS.

1. Spread the sesame seeds on a large plate then dip in the salmon fillets so the top of each is evenly coated. Heat the olive oil in a shallow pan and fry the salmon over a medium heat for 4 minutes on each side or until golden and cooked through. Remove from the heat and drizzle over the roasted sesame oil.

2. Halve the rolls and toast under a broiler. Top each half with some cucumber and red onion. Top with a salmon burger and serve immediately with extra cucumber and red onion.

Pan-fried Salmon
BURGER
WITH MINTED PEA SALSA

1 lb salmon fillet, skinned
4 scallions, finely chopped
1 zucchini, roughly grated
1 cup bread crumbs
1 egg yolk
a little oil, for frying

Minted pea salsa:
1⅓ cups frozen peas
½ red onion, finely chopped
3 tablespoons chopped mint
juice of 1 lime
2 tablespoons olive oil

To serve:
4 crusty rolls
1⅓ cups baby spinach leaves
1 beefsteak tomato, sliced

1. First, make the salsa. Put the peas into a pan of boiling water, bring back to a boil then drain and refresh under cold running water. Blitz in a food processor until finely chopped. Put the chopped peas in a bowl and stir in the rest of the salsa ingredients. Set aside until needed.

2. To make the burger, blitz the salmon fillet in a food processor until finely chopped. Add the remaining burger ingredients and blitz until just mixed but not pureed. With slightly wet hands, divide the mixture into 4 equal portions and form into burgers. Cover and chill for 30 minutes.

3. Heat the oil in a shallow pan and fry the burgers over a medium heat for 4 minutes on each side, until golden brown and cooked through.

4. Halve the rolls and toast under the broiler then top the bases with the baby spinach, tomato slices, and the burgers. Top each burger with some minted pea salsa and serve with the lid on the side.

Swordfish Steak
BURGER
WITH CRUNCHY ORANGE SALSA

1 teaspoon ground cumin
1 teaspoon ground coriander
1 teaspoon paprika
a pinch of ground chili
grated zest of 1 orange
2 tablespoons olive oil
4 swordfish steaks, about 6 oz each
salt and pepper

Crunchy orange salsa:
1 large orange, segmented and finely chopped
3 tablespoons finely chopped flat leaf parsley
1 red chili, finely chopped
3 scallions, finely chopped
3 tablespoons olive oil
3 garlic cloves, finely sliced
1 inch piece of fresh ginger root, peeled and cut into fine matchsticks
1 teaspoon cumin seeds

To serve:
4 sesame seed rolls
mixed salad leaves

1. First make the salsa by mixing together the orange, parsley, chili, and scallions in a bowl. Heat the oil in a skillet and cook the garlic, ginger, and cumin seeds until crisp. Add the contents of the pan to the orange mixture and stir. Set aside until needed.

2. To make the burger, mix together the spices, orange zest, and oil, season with salt and pepper and rub over both sides of the swordfish steaks. Heat a griddle pan or barbecue to medium-high and cook the steaks for 8–10 minutes, turning once, until cooked through.

3. To assemble, halve the rolls, place salad leaves on the base of the rolls, and put the fish steaks on top. Spoon over the orange salsa and top with the roll lid.

CRAB CAKE
BURGER
WITH CORN SALSA

14 oz fresh white crab meat
1 egg, beaten
2 tablespoons mayonnaise
a good pinch of powdered English mustard
2 tablespoons lemon juice
½ red onion, grated
3 tablespoon chives, chopped
a few drops of Tabasco sauce
2½ cups fresh bread crumbs
a little oil, for frying
salt and pepper

Corn salsa:
¾ cup frozen corn kernels
1 small red onion, finely chopped
1 avocado, finely chopped
2 tablespoons chopped chives
1 tablespoon red wine vinegar
2 tablespoons olive oil

To serve:
4 soft rolls
salad leaves

1. In a bowl, combine all the ingredients for the burger, except the bread crumbs, and season lightly with salt and pepper. Divide into 4 equal burgers. Spread the bread crumbs on a plate and coat each burger in them evenly. The mix is very wet so you may need to reshape the burgers in the crumbs. Cover and chill for 1 hour.

2. To make the corn salsa, boil the corn for 2 minutes then drain and refresh under cold running water. Place the corn in a bowl with the red onion, avocado, chives, vinegar, and oil. Season well with salt and pepper and mix thoroughly. Set aside until needed.

3. Heat the oil in a shallow pan and fry the burgers for 2–3 minutes on each side or until heated through and crisp. Drain on paper towels.

4. To assemble, halve the rolls and toast under a broiler. Top each base with a little salad and a burger. Serve with the salsa and the lid on the side.

CORNMEAL-CRUSTED
SHRIMP BURGERS
WITH HARISSA DRESSING

5 oz white fish
14 oz raw jumbo shrimp
3 oz canned water chestnuts, drained and chopped
1 inch piece of fresh ginger root, peeled and grated
6 scallions, finely chopped
1 teaspoon harissa
grated zest of 1 lime
¾ cup cornmeal
a little light olive oil, for frying
salt and pepper

Harissa dressing:
3 teaspoon harissa
3 tablespoons olive oil
juice of 1 lime

To serve:
4 mini pita breads, sliced
1 lime, sliced

1. Skin and bone the fish then place it in a food processor with the shrimp, water chestnuts, ginger, scallions, harissa, lime zest, and a little salt and pepper. Blitz until the mixture comes together but still has a rough texture. Divide the mixture into 8 portions and form into round burgers. Cover and chill for 1 hour.

2. Spread the cornmeal on a large plate. Dip the burgers into the cornmeal and coat evenly. Heat the oil in a shallow pan and fry the burgers for 8 minutes, turning frequently, until cooked through. Meanwhile, beat together the dressing ingredients and set aside.

3. To assemble, wrap the pita bread slices around the burgers, top each one with a slice of lime and secure with a toothpick. Serve accompanied by the harissa dressing.

FALAFEL BURGER

14 oz can chickpeas, drained and rinsed
2 garlic cloves, crushed
1 small red onion, finely chopped
2 teaspoons ground cumin
2 tablespoons chopped cilantro
2 tablespoons chopped flat leaf parsley
grated zest of 1 lemon
1 egg yolk
2 tablespoons gram or all-purpose flour
a little vegetable oil, for frying
salt and pepper

Garlic mint sauce:
¾ cup plain yogurt
2 tablespoons chopped mint
1 garlic clove, crushed

To serve:
8 mini pita breads
6 tablespoons red bell pepper hummus
1 bunch of watercress
2 tomatoes, cut into segments
¼ cucumber, sliced

GRAM FLOUR OR BESAN IS USED IN INDIAN COOKING. IT'S MADE OF GROUND, DRIED CHICKPEAS, WHICH GIVES IT ITS PALE YELLOW COLOR AND HIGH PROTEIN CONTENT. IT'S WORTH GETTING HOLD OF AND KEEPS WELL, REFRIGERATED, FOR UP TO 6 MONTHS. YOU CAN BUY RED BELL PEPPER HUMMUS AT THE DELI COUNTERS OF MOST LARGE SUPERMARKETS.

1. Place all the ingredients for the falafel, except the flour, in a food processor, season with salt and pepper and blitz until ground to a textured paste. Using slightly wet hands, divide the mixture into 8 balls then flatten them slightly to make burgers. Cover and chill for 30 minutes.

2. To make the garlic mint sauce, mix the yogurt with the mint and garlic. Season with salt and pepper and set aside until needed.

3. Lightly coat the burgers with the flour and pan-fry in the oil for 4 minutes on each side until golden brown and crisp.

4. To assemble, toast the pitas under a hot broiler, spread each one with some hummus and top with salad and a burger. Serve with the garlic mint sauce.

SPICY BEAN BURGER

2 tablespoons light olive oil
1 small red onion, finely chopped
2 garlic cloves, crushed
1 yellow bell pepper, cored, seeded,and finely chopped
2 red chilies, seeded and finely chopped
2 teaspoons paprika
1 teaspoon cayenne pepper
½ cup wild arugula, finely chopped
2 tablespoons chopped parsley
1 tablespoon chopped thyme
1 small egg, beaten
1 tablespoon Tabasco sauce
1 cup fresh bread crumbs
2 x 14 oz cans Lima beans, drained and rinsed
a little vegetable oil, for frying
salt and pepper

To serve:
4 soft focaccia rolls
salad leaves
1 quantity Tomato Chili Relish
(*see page 62*)

1. Heat the olive oil in a medium pan and add the onion, garlic, bell pepper, and chilies. Cover and simmer over a low-medium heat for 5 minutes or until the onion is cooked through but not browned. Add the paprika, cayenne pepper, arugula, parsley, and thyme and cook for an additional minute. Remove from the heat and allow to cool.

2. Mix the onion mixture with the remaining burger ingredients and season well with salt and pepper. Mash with a potato masher until well combined. Divide the mixture into 4 portions and form into balls then flatten slightly into burgers. Cover and chill for 30 minutes.

3. Heat some vegetable oil in a shallow nonstick pan and fry the burgers for 3 minutes on each side or until heated through and slightly crisp. Drain well on paper towels.

4. To assemble, halve the rolls and toast under a broiler then top each base with salad leaves and a burger. Serve with the lid and tomato chili relish on the side.

SWEET POTATO, LIMA BEAN, AND FETA BURGER
WITH SUN-BLUSHED TOMATO PESTO

1 lb sweet potatoes, cut into ¾ inch dice
10 oz can Lima beans, drained and rinsed
5 oz feta cheese
2 tablespoons chopped sage
1 tablespoon all-purpose flour
1 egg, beaten
⅔ cup panko or dried bread crumbs
vegetable oil, for frying
salt and pepper

Sun-blushed tomato pesto:
4 oz sun-blushed tomatoes
2 tablespoons roasted pine nuts
3 tablespoons chopped basil leaves
3 tablespoons extra virgin olive oil

To serve:
4 burger buns
salad leaves
toasted pine nuts

1. First, make the pesto by blending together all the pesto ingredients in a small food processor until you have a textured paste.

2. Boil the sweet potatoes in salted boiling water for 15 minutes or until soft. Drain and leave to cool then mash the sweet potatoes with the Lima beans using a potato masher. Fold in the feta and sage and season to taste with salt and pepper, remembering that the feta is quite salty. Divide into 4 portions and form into balls, then flatten slightly into burgers.

3. Coat the burgers in the flour, then dip them first in the beaten egg and then in the bread crumbs. Re-form into a burger shape if necessary and then cover and chill for 30 minutes.

4. Heat the oil in a shallow pan and fry the burgers for 2–3 minutes on each side or until golden brown and crisp. Drain on paper towels.

5. To assemble, halve the buns and toast under a broiler. Top each base with some salad then a burger. Spoon over the pesto and pine nuts and serve immediately with the lid on the side.

CRISPY TOFU
BURGER

13 oz firm tofu
3 tablespoons soy sauce
1 tablespoon rice wine vinegar
1 teaspoon sesame oil
1 inch piece of fresh ginger root, peeled and grated
1 garlic clove, crushed
2 large eggs, beaten
1½ cups fresh bread crumbs
3 tablespoons sesame seeds
a little light olive oil, for frying

Roasted cherry tomatoes:
8 oz cherry tomatoes
2 garlic cloves, chopped
2 tablespoons chopped basil
2 tablespoons olive oil

To serve:
4 crusty rolls
salad leaves

1. Cut the tofu into 4 square pieces and lay them flat in a non-metallic dish. Mix together the soy sauce, vinegar, sesame oil, ginger, and garlic and pour over the tofu. Cover and leave to marinate for at least 1 hour, but preferably over night.

2. To cook the roasted cherry tomatoes, place the tomatoes into a roasting pan and scatter with the garlic, basil, and olive oil. Cook in a preheated oven, 400°F, until the skins start to split, about 15 minutes. Set aside until needed (the tomatoes can be eaten hot or at room temperature).

3. To make the burgers, dip the tofu into the beaten egg, then into the bread crumbs and finally into the sesame seeds. Dip each burger in the egg, then the bread crumbs again for an extra thick coating.

4. Heat the oil in a shallow pan and fry the tofu burgers on each side over a medium-high heat until golden and crispy, about 6–8 minutes. Drain on paper towels.

5. To assemble, halve the rolls and toast under a broiler. Top each base with salad leaves and a crispy tofu burger. Spoon over the roasted cherry tomatoes and their juices and serve immediately with the lids on the side.

PORTOBELLO MUSHROOM BURGER
WITH GOAT CHEESE

PORTOBELLO MUSHROOMS ARE LARGE, FLAT MUSHROOMS. THEY HAVE A DENSE, MEATY TEXTURE AND RUSTIC FLAVOR THAT IS PERFECT FOR THIS BURGER.

4 portobello mushrooms
2 garlic cloves, finely chopped
2 tablespoons chopped thyme
3 tablespoons olive oil
4 large slices of roasted red bell pepper
5 oz goat cheese, cut into 4 thick slices
2–4 tablespoons butter
2 cups fresh bread crumbs
grated zest of 1 lemon
4 tablespoons finely chopped parsley
salt and pepper

To serve:
2 large burger buns
1½ cups arugula leaves, plus extra for garnish

1. Place the mushrooms in a roasting pan and sprinkle them with the garlic and thyme. Drizzle over the olive oil and cook in a preheated oven, 400°F, for 10 minutes.

2. Place a slice of bell pepper and a slice of goat cheese on each mushroom. Heat the butter in a nonstick skillet and fry the bread crumbs, lemon zest, and parsley until the bread crumbs just start to brown, about 3 minutes. Spoon the bread crumb mixture over the mushrooms and season well with salt and pepper. Return the burgers to the oven and roast for a further 5 minutes until the top is golden and the cheese has started to melt.

3. To assemble, halve the buns and toast under a broiler. Top each half with arugula leaves and a mushroom. Garnish with extra arugula and serve.

Red Cabbage

COLESLAW WITH TOASTED
ALMONDS AND WHOLEGRAIN MUSTARD DRESSING

¼ red cabbage
1 small red onion, finely sliced
1 carrot, grated
1 orange bell pepper, cored, seeded, and shredded
½ cup sliced almonds, dry roasted
salt and pepper

Wholegrain mustard dressing:
juice of 1 orange
1 tablespoon wholegrain mustard
1 garlic clove, crushed
3 tablespoons olive oil

1. Remove the core and outer leaves from the cabbage and finely shred with a sharp knife or push through the shredder attachment on a food processor. In a large bowl, mix the cabbage with the onion, carrot, bell pepper, and almonds.

2. Beat together all the ingredients for the dressing and toss with the shredded vegetables. Season well with salt and pepper and allow to stand for 30 minutes before serving.

CAJUN SWEET POTATO FRIES

2 sweet potatoes, finely sliced
4 tablespoons cornstarch
2 tablespoons Cajun seasoning
a little vegetable oil, for deep frying

1. Place the sweet potato slices in a large bowl and add the cornstarch and Cajun seasoning. Toss together well to lightly coat the fries.

2. Quarter-fill a large pan with vegetable oil and heat it to 350° or until a piece of bread browns in 30 seconds. Fry the potatoes in batches for 2 minutes or until golden and crisp. Drain on lots of paper towels.

STRAW PARSNIP FRIES
WITH THYME

2 large parsnips
1 teaspoon dried thyme
1 tablespoon all-purpose flour
vegetable oil, for deep-frying

1. Slice the parsnips very thinly, preferably using a mandolin with a thin julienne blade. Put the parsnip fries in a bowl and toss with the dried thyme and flour.

2. Quarter-fill a large pan with vegetable oil and heat to 350°F or until a piece of bread browns in 30 seconds. Fry the parsnips in batches for 2 minutes or until golden and crisp. Drain on lots of paper towels.

GARLIC AND ROSEMARY-FLAVORED THICK CUT FRIES

1 lb red potatoes
6 garlic cloves, skins on
3 tablespoons olive oil
2 tablespoons chopped rosemary
rock salt and pepper

1. Cut the potatoes into thick fries and put them in a large nonstick roasting pan. Crush the garlic cloves in their skins and scatter over the fries. Drizzle with the olive oil, scatter over the rosemary and season with rock salt and pepper. Cook in a preheated oven, 400°F, for 40 minutes, giving the fries a good shake every 10 minutes to prevent them from sticking.

2. When the fries are crisp and golden remove them from the oven, drain on paper towels and serve immediately.

SOUTHERN FRIED ONION RINGS

3 onions, cut into ¼ inch rings
2 cups thick buttermilk
1 cup all-purpose flour
2 teaspoons sweet or ordinary paprika
1 teaspoon cayenne pepper
1 teaspoon freshly ground pepper
1 teaspoon rock salt
vegetable oil, for deep frying

1. Place the onion rings in a large bowl and pour over the buttermilk. Allow to marinate for at least 30 minutes.

2. Mix together the flour, paprika, cayenne pepper, ground pepper, and salt on a plate.

3. Quarter-fill a large pan with vegetable oil and heat to 350°F or until a piece of bread browns in 30 seconds.

4. Remove a small handful of onion rings from the buttermilk and coat in the seasoned flour. Cook the rings in the oil for 2 minutes or until golden brown. Drain well on paper towels and serve warm.

FENNEL AND
ORANGE
SALAD

USING AN AGED VINEGAR WILL GIVE MUCH MORE DEPTH OF FLAVOR WITHOUT ADDING OVERPOWERING ACIDITY. IT'S A PRODUCT THAT'S WELL WORTH HAVING IN YOUR PANTRY.

1 large head endive
1 large head radicchio
2 small fennel bulbs
3 oranges, segmented
½ pomegranate

Dressing:
3 tablespoons olive oil
1 tablespoon aged red wine vinegar
1 tablespoon honey
salt and pepper

1. To make the dressing, beat together the olive oil, vinegar, and honey. Season with salt and pepper and set aside until needed.

2. Separate the endive and radicchio into leaves and arrange on a large platter. Finely slice the fennel and layer with the orange segments over the salad leaves.

3. Drizzle over the dressing, scatter with the pomegranate seeds and serve.

ASIAN SALAD

1 bunch of scallions, shredded
⅔ cup bean sprouts
3 Baby Gem lettuces, leaves separated
1 cucumber, cut into ribbons with a vegetable peeler
1 small bunch of mint, torn
1 small bunch of basil, torn
1 small bunch of cilantro, torn

Dressing:
2 tablespoons light olive oil
grated zest and juice of 1 lime
1 large red chili, seeded and finely chopped
1 tablespoon Asian fish sauce
1 tablespoon light soy sauce
a pinch of sugar

THE FISH SAUCE IN THIS DRESSING GIVES THE SALAD AN AUTHENTIC ASIAN FLAVOR. YOU CAN USE NAM PLA, NUOC MAM, OR NUOC NAM AND CAN FIND IT IN MOST SUPERMARKETS OR SPECIALTY ASIAN MARKETS.

1. Place the shredded scallions and bean sprouts in iced water and leave for 30 minutes, then remove and drain well.

2. In a large serving bowl, toss the onion and sprouts with the lettuce leaves, cucumber, and herbs.

3. Beat together the ingredients for the dressing in a small bowl and pour over the salad. Serve immediately.

Tomato Ketchup

MAKING YOUR OWN KETCHUP TAKES A LITTLE TIME BUT THE LACK OF ARTIFICIAL SWEETENERS AND PRESERVATIVES MAKES A FAR SUPERIOR SAUCE AND IS WELL WORTH THE EFFORT.

6 lb ripe tomatoes, roughly chopped
1 onion, chopped
1 garlic clove, chopped
1 red bell pepper, seeded and chopped
1 cup cider vinegar
1 cup sugar
1 tablespoon green peppercorns
1 teaspoon salt
1 teaspoon powdered English mustard
½ teaspoon ground allspice
½ teaspoon cayenne pepper
¼ teaspoon ground cloves or
5 whole cloves

1. Place all the ingredients into a heavy saucepan and bring to a boil. Simmer over a medium heat for 35 minutes, stirring frequently.

2. Remove the pan from the heat, cover and let rest for 1–2 hours. This will allow the flavors to blend together.

3. Push the mixture through a fine strainer, discarding the mushy skins left in the strainer. Wash out the pan and pour in the strained tomato mixture. Bring back to a boil and simmer the ketchup over a low heat until thick, about 1½ hours, stirring occasionally.

4. Pour the ketchup into dry sterilized bottles or jars, seal, and cool. Use immediately or store for up to 1 month in the refrigerator.

MAYONNAISE

2 large egg yolks
1 teaspoon powdered English mustard
a good pinch of salt
1–2 tablespoons lemon juice
¾ cup peanut oil
½ cup olive oil

1. Beat together the yolks, mustard, salt, and lemon juice in a bowl, preferably one with a narrow base. Place the bowl on a damp cloth, to help hold it steady, so you have a free hand to pour in the oil. Alternatively, use a blender.

2. When the yolks have blended start adding the oils a few drops at a time, beating well between each addition. Once the mixture starts to thicken, you can start pouring the oil in a very thin, steady stream. If the mayonnaise curdles, simply beat another yolk in a clean bowl and slowly add the curdled sauce to it, beating continuously. If you are using a blender, gradually add the oil while blending at the same time.

3. When you have added all the oil, check the taste and consistency, adding lemon juice for sharpness and salt and mustard to taste. For a lighter consistency, beat in 1–2 tablespoons of boiling water.

Additional Flavors

Garlic or Aïoli Add 5 crushed garlic cloves to the yolk mixture before you start adding the oil.

Dijon or Wholegrain Mustard Add 1 tablespoon of either Dijon or wholegrain mustard to the yolk mixture before you start adding the oil. Stir through more mustard at the end, to taste.

Mixed Herbs Stir 4 tablespoons freshly chopped mixed herbs, such as parsley, chives, and basil, into the finished mayonnaise.

Basil Stir 4 tablespoons freshly chopped basil into the finished mayonnaise.

Lemon Stir 2 tablespoons grated lemon zest through the mixture. Add a few drops of lemon juice to lighten the mixture.

Horseradish Stir 1 tablespoon creamed horseradish through the finished mayonnaise.

MAKES 1½ CUPS • PREPARATION TIME: 20 MINUTES • COOKING TIME: 25 MINUTES

SMOKY
PEPPER RELISH

2 red bell peppers, cored, halved, and seeded
1 yellow bell pepper, cored, halved, and seeded
2 tablespoons chopped basil
1½ tablespoons balsamic vinegar
3 tablespoons olive oil
3 garlic cloves, sliced
1 teaspoon smoked paprika
salt and pepper

1. Broil the peppers under a hot broiler until the skins are black. Transfer to a heatproof bowl and cover with plastic wrap. Allow to cool then peel off and discard the skins.

2. Finely slice the peppers and put them into a bowl with the basil and balsamic vinegar.

3. Heat the oil and fry the garlic and paprika until the garlic is just starting to brown then pour the oil over the peppers. Season with salt and pepper and mix well. Spoon into a sterilized jar and use immediately or store it in the refrigerator for up to a week.

MAKES 1¼ CUPS • PREPARATION TIME: 15 MINUTES • COOKING TIME: 45 MINUTES

Tomato
CHILI RELISH

5 large red chilies, seeded and chopped
3 garlic cloves, chopped
1 lb tomatoes, diced
½ cup sugar
½ cup red wine vinegar

1. Place the chilies, garlic, and half the tomatoes in a food processor and blitz until pureed.

2. Pour the puree into a large heavy pan with the sugar, vinegar, and remaining tomatoes. Bring to a boil and simmer for about 40–45 minutes or until thick, stirring occasionally. Set aside to cool slightly.

3. Pour the relish into sterilized jars and seal. This relish will keep in the refrigerator for up to 2 weeks.

LIMA BEAN, TOMATO, AND CILANTRO SALSA

10 oz can Lima beans, drained and rinsed
3 medium plum tomatoes, diced
1 large red chili, seeded and finely chopped
1 large green chili, seeded and finely chopped
2 garlic cloves, finely chopped
juice and grated zest of 1 lime
2 tablespoons olive oil
3 tablespoons chopped cilantro
salt and pepper

1. Mix the Lima beans with all the remaining ingredients and season well with salt and pepper. Allow to infuse for 30 minutes then serve.

QUICK BBQ SAUCE

THIS CLASSIC SAUCE WILL GO WITH MOST BURGERS. CHIPOTLE TABASCO SAUCE, IF YOU CAN FIND IT, HAS A SMOKY YET SUBTLE CHILI FLAVOR WHICH WORKS WELL IN THIS RECIPE.

1 cup tomato ketchup
½ cup tomato paste
½ cup apple cider vinegar
4 tablespoons blackstrap molasses
1 tablespoon Worcestershire sauce
1 teaspoon Dijon mustard
1 teaspoon Tabasco sauce (or Chipotle Tabasco)

1. Place all ingredients in a saucepan and simmer over a medium heat for 5–10 minutes or until thick. Pour into sterilized jars and allow to cool. Use immediately or store in the refrigerator for up to 2 weeks.

INDEX